THE SLED SURPRISE

All inquiries should be addressed to:
Barron's Educational Series, Inc.
250 Wireless Boulevard
Hauppauge, NY 11788

International Standard Book Number 0-8120-4677-3

Library of Congress Catalog Card Number 91-566

Library of Congress Cataloging-in-Publication Data

Erickson, Gina Clegg.
    The sled surprise / Gina Clegg Erickson and Kelli C. Foster :
illustrations by Kerri Gifford.
        p. cm.—(Get ready...get set...read!)
Summary: Ned and Ted build their own sled.
    ISBN: 0-8120-4677-3
    (1. Sleds—Fiction   2. Stories in rhyme.)
I. Foster, Kelli C.   II. Gifford, Kerri, ill.   III. Title.   IV. Series: Erickson,
Gina Clegg. Get ready...get set...read!
PZ8.3.E787Sl 1991
(E)—dc20   91–566
                                                   CIP
                                                   AC

PRINTED IN HONG KONG

234   9927   98765432

GET READY...GET SET...READ!

THE SLED SURPRISE

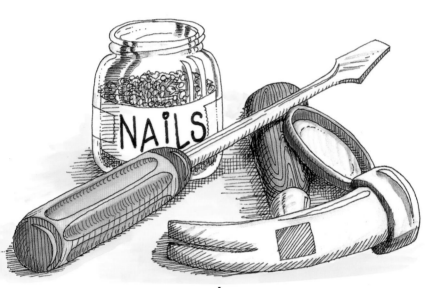

by
Foster & Erickson

Illustrations by
Kerri Gifford

FOREST HOUSE™
School & Library Edition

Ned, Ted, and E

aw Jed and his red sled.

They had no sled.

Come in the shed.
Let's make a sled!

What kind of sled?

We can use the bed!

A bed-sled?

Can Ned and Te

make a sled?

Yes, they can!

The first bed-sled.

Down they spe

n the first bed-sled.

Ned, Ted, and Ed
sped by Jed.

The End

The ED Word Family

Ed
Ned
Ted
Jed
red
bed
sled
sped
bed-sled
shed

Sight Words

a
by
of
saw
the
come
down
kind
they
what
first

Dear Parents and Educators:

Welcome to *Get Ready...Get Set...Read!*

We've created these books to introduce children to the magic of reading.

Each story in the series is built around one or two word families. For example, *A Mop for Pop* uses the OP word family. Letters and letter blends are added to OP to form words such as TOP, LOP, and STOP. As you can see, once children are able to read OP, it is a simple task for them to read the entire word family. In addition to word families, we have used a limited number of "sight words." These are words found to occur with high frequency in the books your child will soon be reading. Being able to identify sight words greatly increases reading skill.

You might find the steps outlined on the facing page useful in guiding your work with your beginning reader.

We had great fun creating these books, and great pleasure sharing them with our children. We hope *Get Ready...Get Set...Read!* helps make this first step in reading fun for you and your new reader.

Kelli C. Foster, PhD
Educational Psychologist

Gina Clegg Erickson, MA
Reading Specialist

Guidelines for Using *Get Ready...Get Set...Read!*

Step 1. Read the story to your child.

Step 2. Have your child read the Word Family list aloud several times.

Step 3. Invent new words for the list. Print each new combination for your child to read. Remember, nonsense words can be used (*dat, kat, gat*).

Step 4. Read the story *with* your child. He or she reads all of the Word Family words; you read the rest.

Step 5. Have your child read the Sight Word list aloud several times.

Step 6. Read the story *with* your child again. This time he or she reads the words from both lists; you read the rest.

Step 7. Your child reads the entire book to you!

Titles in the
Get Ready...Get Set...Read! Series